Octopuses & Other Sea Creatures

by Becci Louise

A collection of poems and photographs from the

Octopuses & Other Sea Creatures

audiovisual installation & performance, staged

in Portsmouth Cathedral in November 2022.

A Kino Kult Dérive

A One Thousand Plateaus Paperback

Octopuses & Other Sea Creatures

by

Becci Louise

First published 2024 by Kino Kult CIC

ISBN: 978-1-913001-08-7

Design by Vaani Parekh & Photos by Jesse Beale

Preface

In early 2019 I was invited to participate in a commission for an immersive theatre show from the New Theatre Royal for their Festival of the Sea. The producer of the show, John Sackett wanted to work with musicians, poets, performers, and dancers to out together an immersive show in The Square Tower, Portsmouth. The show was to be an interpretation of a book of poem-stories entitled Octopus Medicine by Becci Louise. The three verse stories in the book call us down into another world, the world of the octopus where we meet an octopus who dreams of stars, a self-important fisherman who gets what's coming to him, and a misunderstood monster. What is interesting about these tales is that they position you as the octopus who experiences man as the monster, a reversal of the usual nature as monster narrative. John invited me to come on board as an audiovisual artist and to light up the interior of The Square Tower with video projections. This I did and Octopuses & Other Sea Creatures was born.

The event was very successful and sold out all eighty available tickets. It involved a choir, a narrator, actors, dancers, a sonic artist, spoken word and me with my projectors, casting an undersea environment about the walls of the space within which the story could unfold. John and I had been working together for some time and increasingly we had been working towards more immersive events fusing performance, sound, and video to create live experiences. This staging of Octopuses and Other Sea Creatures not only saw the coming together of a broad range of different creative practices it was also a commission. For me it seemed like a real success. But for me it deserved more than just one night in front of 80 people, I felt that it deserved to be bigger, more elaborate and for a bigger audience. With John's blessing I set about applying for funding to develop the show as a year-long project with the intention of staging a large-scale audiovisual experience for the second iteration of the We Shine Portsmouth - Festival of Light.

The intention for the second iteration of the project was to create a stunning immersive light and sound experience that would take the audience on a journey deep undersea to experience the magic of the ocean,

explore its depths, and meet the Octopus. The journey would be narrated
through spoken word, challenging the audience to rethink our relationship
to the oceans and to think of the octopus, not as a monster from the deep,
but as a companion species, as a co-inhabitant of this planet. We wanted
audiences to develop a connection with the ocean and recognise that
the sea is not only our birthplace, but an ecosystem on which our own,
terrestrial lives, thoroughly rely. At the same time, we were aware that
Portsmouth has a symbiotic relationship with the sea and would not exist
without it. Generations of local people owe their livelihoods to the ocean,
having served in, or helped service the Royal Navy, fished in local waters,
or worked in our tourism industry. Could stories about octopus-human
relations reframe our historical and cultural narratives about the octopus.
This is the question we set out to answer. The funding application was
successful and in January 2022 we initiated the project with a launch event
in collaboration with The Front Room led by John Sackett. Inviting spoken
word artists and musicians to respond to Octopus Medicine we presented
a night of sea-shaped spoken words, and maritime musical musings.
Following on from this we released aseries of podcasts featuring Becci
Louise reading from Octopus Medicine with accompanying soundscape. We
ran a series creative writing workshop's for adults and young people as part
of Portsmouth Bookfest that spring. We partnered with researchers from
University of Portsmouth to place "researchers-in-the-classroom" alongside
artists and callenged them to create artworks about the "pollution we don't
see" for an exhibition in a local church. The exhibition happened on World
Ocean Day and included another evening of music, dance, and storytelling,
with a talk by a professional Octopus Keeper from Bristol Aquarium. There
was a summer school at Groundlings Theatre with workshops in immersive
theatre, video projection and sonic art. All of which fed into the final show
planned for November in Portsmouth Cathedral.

During the development of the show the creative team Kim Balouch
(video), Rusty Sheriff (sound design) and Angela Parks (Project Manager),
encouraged by our mentors Thomas Buckley and Joe Hufton, were seeking
a means for structuring the experience for the audience. We knew that
we wanted to take people on a deep dive undersea to meet the octopus,
but we needed a way of narrating that experience. Talking with Becci,
we both agreed we didn't want to explore the story from the perspective

of the original 2019 show which had embraced Lovecraftian nightmare of Cthulhu as its central narrative. Instead, we wanted to return to the original verse stories and work in dialogue with them to explore a more compassionate relationship between nature and culture. Our desire was to change the audience's perception of the octopus as a monster or as something alien, something to be frightened of. Fostering instead a perception of the octopus as a companion species to which we are bonded. As a starting point we asked ourselves what are the eight lessons the octopuses could teach us and this is what we came up with.

The Eight Lessons of the Octopus

Tune into nature – Lean into the world, becoming-with
our companion species, staying with the trouble, seeing
ourselves in the octopus and other sea creatures.

Camouflage – An octopus melds with its environment, blending with its surroundings, adapting quickly to new situations. It becomes a part of its world. I think we can learn, from the octopus, how to integrate ourselves back into the natural world without harming it or ourselves. An octopus lives in harmony with its habitat. We need to learn to do the same.

Curiosity and play – Octopuses love to learn. They are endlessly curious, they love to play, they solve problems and investigate the world, we can learn and research about nature so that we can live in harmony. I think we need to learn to be more curious and playful.

Slow down and live fully – Octopuses are generally solitary creatures. They are comfortable in their own company. While humans are biologically and psychologically more inclined towards a social nature, I think there's still a lot we can learn from the octopus' solitary nature. It' comfortable in it's own company. It doesn't mind the quiet. It knows how to be calm, to be slow, to take it's time. In a social structure that expects us to be connected and on the go all the time, I think we can learn from the octopus how to stand still, breathe in, and be with and by ourselves.

Recycling, Construction & Imagination – Octopuses like to rearrange their dens and decorate, they reuse discarded items, teaching us to reuse what we have. Octopuses build. They're imaginative. And they build based on their surroundings. We need to think like the octopus does, to think beyond ourselves, to imagine meaningfully, sustainably, compassionately.

Collaboration – An octopus has whole body awareness; it has nine brains (one central brain, and one brain in each arm). There is so much neurological matter in each of their arms that scientists have speculated each arm might have its own personality. We can also learn to collaborate with others and work together as a team to solve the worlds environmental problems.

Communication – The octopus has 360 degree vision with their eyes, they can teach us to look at the larger picture of how our actions affect the ocean. An octopus also talks with its whole body. It uses colour, gesture, and texture to communicate with others, and it understands language with its whole body, too. As humans, we also talk with our whole bodies. With our faces, our hands, our stance, as well as our voices. Somewhere, we seem to have lost the ability to read each other as wholly as the octopus does. I think this is something the octopus can help us re-learn.

Compassion/Passion – An octopus has three hearts. They are solitary creatures, and yet they are known to befriend humans. Octopuses in captivity are often very affectionate with their keepers, and there are stories of wild octopus that make friends with humans. We need to learn from the octopus how to make proper, meaningful relationships with species outside our own. Relationships that are more than master/human and pet/animal. We need to learn to communicate on an equal level with the other lifeforms around us.

Becci turned these lessons into new series of poems, The Song of Octopus, which we then used as the narrative foundation for the audio visual experience we staged in Portsmouth Cathedral over three nights in November 2022. It is these poems alongside images captured from the show that are presented here in this book. Before you go on to read the poems and look at the images from our show, I will leave you with this thought. The octopus has long been seen as a threat to seafarers, a monster, an alien species. But what if it is really our friend, a companion species? – If we listen carefully, what story will it tell us?

Dr. Roy Hanney (Producer)
https://octopusstory.com/

An introduction
from Becci Louise

Octopus Stories Introduction

In 2017, I published a collection of poems with Two Rivers Press, a small independent poetry publisher based in Reading. This collection was a series of three stories about octopuses. Yes, you read that right.

Somehow, I persuaded a serious poetry publisher, most of whose poets were over the age of fifty, to publish three narrative verses about octopuses. I still see this as a significant lifetime achievement. This collection became Octopus Medicine, the inspiration behind the Octopuses and Other Sea Creatures project, and these stories.

Why octopuses?

The octopus is a shapeshifter, A master of disguise and misdirection. She is highly intelligent, playful, innovative and inventive. She uses tools. She is curious. She delights in puzzles and challenges.

She is also a mystery. We know so little about the sea, and the octopus represents typical features that we consider monstrous and repulsive; she's boneless, slimy, tentacular. Her body is almost alien in both appearance and anatomy. Her blood is blue, pumped by three hearts.

She has a beak like a parrot and a brain shaped like a doughnut, which wraps around her esophagus. She has enough neurological matter in each of her tentacles that, technically speaking, she has nine brains. Some biologists believe that each of her arms might even contain enough neurons for each to have its own distinct personality. Imagine each of your limbs having its own character, making its own decisions, developing likes and dislikes.

The octopus is also a solitary creature, and yet we know of incredible stories in which an octopus will form a powerful bond with a human being. She is, arguably, a symbol for everything about the sea that we fear when we should love, that we fight when we should embrace, and that we destroy when we should protect. Octopuses and Other Sea Creatures was a project that focused on this conflicting relationship we have with the sea. Our treatment of it, and reliance on it, are at complete odds with each other. As a coastal town, Portsmouth's relationship with the sea is direct and intense. It will be at the forefront of rising sea levels and worsening storms as the climate crisis takes hold, but it is also a bustling harbour town and port, a naval base, and a trading route. There has been talk of building sea walls in vulnerable areas, barricading the sea out. I understand this fear of the sea, how its power and unpredictability can cause extreme damage to homes and lives.

But the sea, like many areas of our planet, is in pain. A pain the human species caused.

Its creatures suffocate on our waste, are poisoned by our rubbish, disturbed by our huge freighters, displaced by warming waters, and hunted and slaughtered in their masses.

I would argue it's time, not to lock the sea out, but to invite it in, have a conversation with it. The sea deserves our love, our respect, and our protection.

These stories are the beginning of that conversation. A call to arms for those brave enough to wade into the shallows and invite the sea to commune with them. To ask its forgiveness and begin to heal our broken relationship with it.

There are many things we can do to rebuild our fractured friendship with the sea. Eating responsibly sourced seafood is a good start, but also considering how we dispose of our rubbish, seeking out plastic free alternatives for household staples, making clear to our MPs and leaders that managing the climate crisis is of utmost importance to us, the voters. But above all, we can teach the next generation about the wonders of the sea.

Show it to your children. Build their wonder for the ocean and its life. It will take an army to overcome the challenges we face, but that army needs to march not with spears and swords, but with kindness. We need an army of wardens. Stewards. Keepers. People who will help the sea heal when it is crying out for mercy.

Read these stories with compassion in your heart. And remember the octopus. She is watching.

Becci Louise
Writer

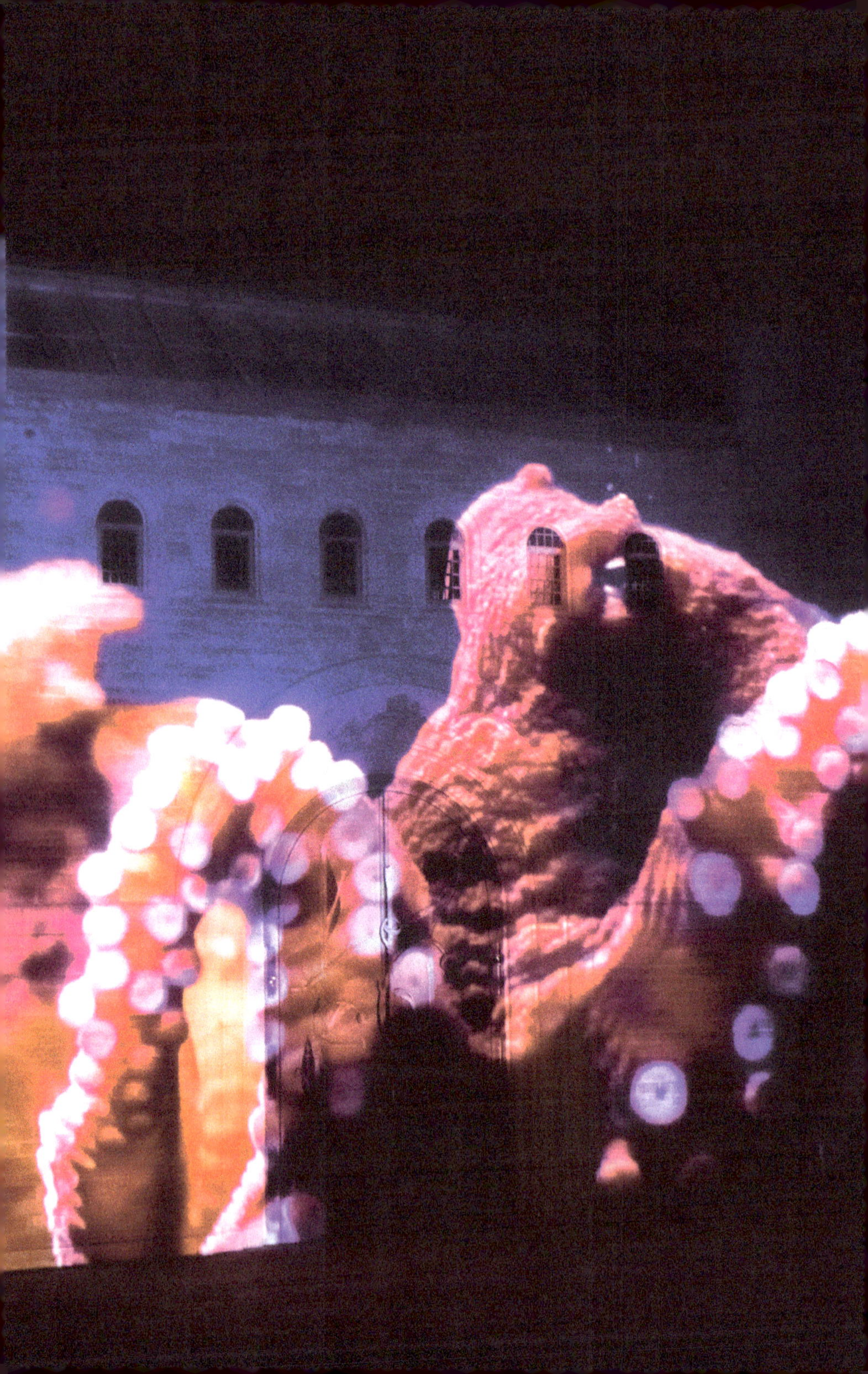

Songs of the octopus

Song of the Dark
Tune into Nature

Listen.
To the tremor of fish tails.
To the song of the deep,
sung in vibration and light.
Listen to this hell-dark,
this bone-crushing, life-giving blackness,
this endless,
velvet
saline paradise.
We speak in heartbeats,
ultra-violet and infra-red.
Learn our language quickly,
learn the first rule of the deep.
Beware the lights.
Here, the dark is your safety,
a swaddling of night to wrap you in shadow.
So hold tight to this dark while you travel down here,
while you kick your human feet,
breathe the human air you bring down with you,
try to keep your brittle human bodies from breaking
beneath these miles and miles and miles of ancient water.
There are monsters above you and monsters below you
and they have been prowling these depths since the world was young.
They have seen asteroids fall and continents shatter,
they have seen the world end again and again
and they have survived.
We have survived.
Scared yet? You should be.
Because you are not in charge here.
This hell-dark, tooth-ridden, lung-screaming world

is not yours but *ours*.
A tentacular arm reaches from the dark,
Touching, searching. Do you recoil?
Maybe. But this is a friend.
This is your guide. The Changer.
The Trickster. The Explorer.
This is the octopus.
Her many arms will hold you safely down here.
Her colours will be your language.
Listen.
She has much to tell you.
Remember that, while you're down here.
Whatever bounty you take,
whatever lessons you learn,
remember these things were given.
A gift of treaty. Of truce.
Because the ocean has been here since the planet was born
and it will be here long after your kind are gone.
But we are weary of this battle,
Of the toxins in our waters, the bleaching of our reefs.
You cannot—will not—break us.
And so we offer you this:
Come down and understand.
You have forty minutes of oxygen.
Forty minutes in the dark.
And these many voices have things to teach.
So, listen.

Song of the Reef
Camouflage

Lift into the ocean swell,
tails and fins, questing mouths.
Feel the silent pulse of the reef,
its catch-and-eat, hide-and-live laws.

The quiet, brutal battle of the coral,
devouring each other, an insatiable army.
We know that our survival means we must kill,
consume, destroy.

Beneath these rocks, the bones of fish

drift like seaweed on the tide,
and at night, frightened fish hide
in rocky dens from the ragged mouths of sharks,
who scent flesh on the moonlit current.

Life at the cusp of ending,
life in the thrill of survival.
Life, quick and sharp
and always wanting more.

But listen deeper. Hear that?
The brilliance of new life. Fish eggs
Waiting under rocks,
The vibrant colours, the love of life.

Because, although this place is brutal,
We love it here. This is our strength.
The innovation of biology.
Watch the Japanese Pufferfish

build his masterpiece in the sand,

symmetry. Transient art,
an act of worship for his female,
for the future.

See how clownfish caress
the stinging tentacles of anemones.
A friendship born of millennia,
truce. Symbiosis.

The reef understands co-operation.

How to take just what is needed.
How to dance in the flash of sun,
How to dodge teeth, strike bargains.
And how to alter ourselves

To fit with what the ocean needs.

Song of the Shallows
Curiosity and Play

White-caps crest in a dancing breeze
And we ride the tide,
leap, porpoise, prance over the border
between sea and air.
Dolphins drawing arches against the sky,
Sealions leap and twist,
Fish gather in vast shoals at the surface,
Turning the water black.
           Because we know what lurks beneath.
Hungry mouths, cutting teeth.
      So we prance and play
Because it's good to be alive.
      Even the sharks gather close to the surface,
Their sinuous bodies ooze and twist,
Drawing effortless lines through the currents.
      Marlin flash their scales against the sunlight,
Driving their sword-mouths, cutting the water.
And above, seabirds dive,
      screaming, after the silver bullets of fish.
We are life. Curious and playful,
      Pressing at the portal between sea and air,
Living fast. Living free.

Song of the Spineless
Slow down and live fully

Careful where you tread.
This ocean floor is home to the boneless ones,
the unrelenting keepers of the dark,
their exoskeletons crunching in shark jaws.
They are soft-shelled, slow-limbed,
living like time is something elastic
that stretches the length of evolution.
    And the pulse of their mouths,
  their toothless maws,
unspooling the dead things left to rot
  on the white sand,
    is the timepiece of the deep,
     a measure of endings.
       The miniature and the monstrous
   who know their end will be a clash of teeth.
   So they wait. Hungry,
  in dark crevices of rock,
clinging to the undersides of reefs,
  patient as moonlight.

And every so often.
  The flash of lights. A visual shout.
   Ultra-violet pulses in the dark.
    The Vampire Squid dancing,
  her arms awash with light,
her mantle oozing, fluttering
  flamenco of the deep.
   And there, an arthropod flash,
    The lightshow of commingling.
  A kaleidoscope of existence,

 Spineless things live slowly.
  Know how to watch, to wait.

But with their dancing lights,
their brief burst of colour,
they know, too, how to turn the ocean into art
with their living, luminescent paint.

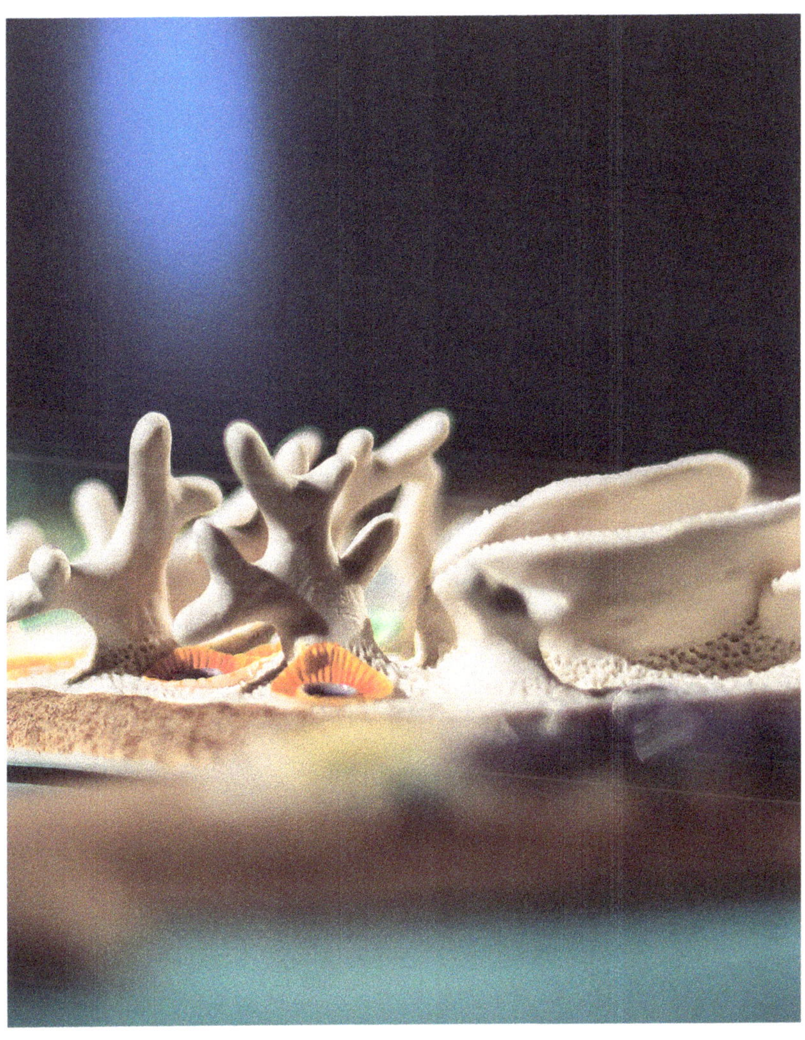

Song of the Kelp Forests
Recycling, Restructuring and Imagination

Swim carefully, here.
      The kelp grows huge and strong,
its bulbous, air-filled sacs dragging it skyward.
If it catches you, it wraps tight.
Keep hold of the octopus' arm.
      She knows these ever-moving forests.
They are a part of her, as they should be a part of you.
The kelp drifts in the soft ocean current,
tendrils gently reaching.
      Here, we know how to live through dreams.
Building lairs from old rope and plastic,
      wrapping our eggs in kelp.
We know how to use our environment,
      build a home from rubbish and debris,
      make armour from shells and rocks.
Because, here, the eyes are always hungry
and we live through ingenuity.
      Our world gives everything we need.
      All we need to do
         is imagine it.
            And we imagine beyond survival.
The octopus leads you down to her lair,
To the carefully curated garden she's made there.
      Shells, laid large to small,
      The empty sac of a shark's egg, wedged beneath a stone,
      The plastic frays of discarded string,
Planted like roses in the sand.
She bids you touch it gently.
      For this is an expression of her.
        A declaration of sentience.
    This is a moment of self.
A reminder the ocean is full of people, too.
People with fins and teeth and tentacles.

People who are beyond human.
    Who can create for the sake of creating,
Who can love to live, even as the living is hard.

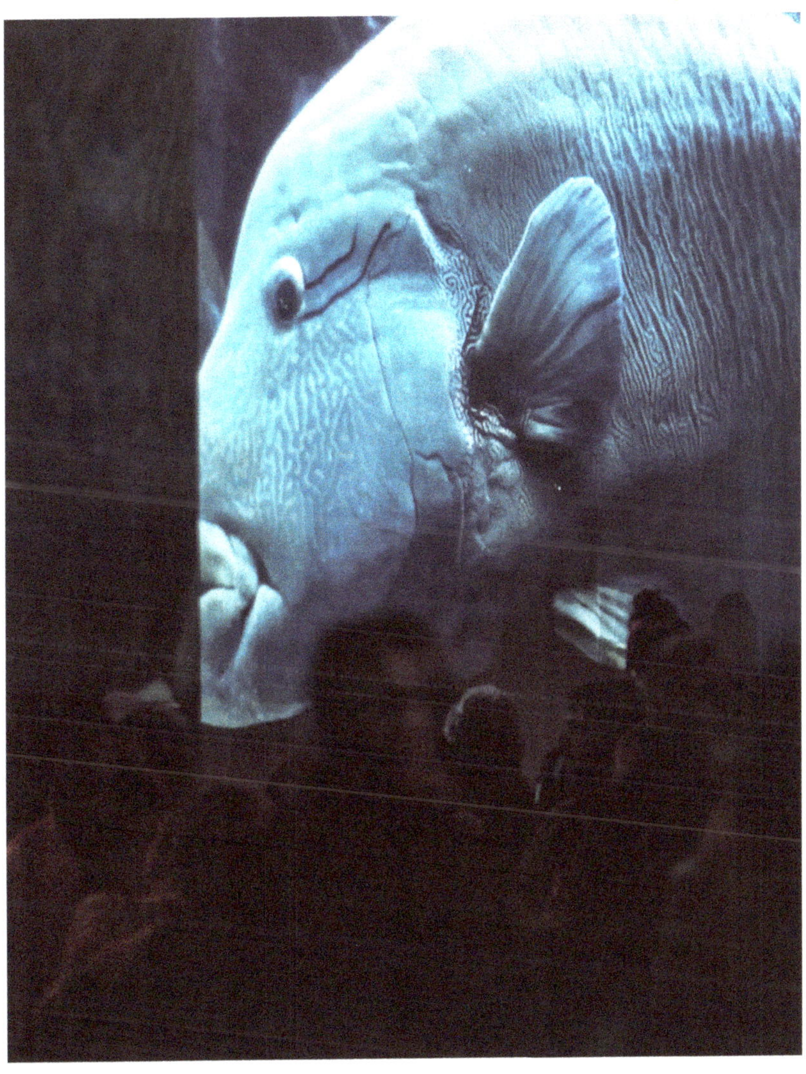

Song of the Wandering Shoals
Collaboration

Flash of fish, silver shimmer on the blue tide.
We are a multitude.
A thousand, thousand lithe bodies
writhing through the blue.
We are the march of the ocean,
our shining bodies throwing light,
a kaleidoscope of movement,
darting and rolling,
travelling ever onwards.
The sheer number of us means safety.
        A collaboration of survival.
Because without each other,
we would die.
        Sound familiar?
Feel the cold softness of the octopus paw
holding your hand.
Squeezing,
        Drawing you into the shoals,
into the song of the ocean.
To be part of this dance.
Because you
are
part of this dance.
        The endless life-death-life cycle of the world.
Driven by the ocean.
The engine of the Earth.
        Remember your ancestors crawled from this ocean.
And we go back to the ocean.
To this dance.

Song of the Coastal Tide
Communication (a border between worlds)

The tide is like breath.
In.
      Out.
Curling white in the high wind,
Rolling blue in the stillness.
      Sandpipers forage in the shallows,
      Racing the oncoming water.
Oysters clean the current.
Silver fish flash in the morning sun.
The ocean calls and the land answers.
      Because there is no answer without an ask,
There is no language without listening.
You have stopped listening,
      So half the song of the world falls silent.
Listen, to the whisper-kiss of water on sand.
      To the endless call of gulls circling overhead.
      To the crackle of crab claws
      To the pucker and pull of seaweed.
Listen.
In.
      Out.
The tide is like a breath.

Song of the Old Ocean Gods
Compassion and Passion

We sense you down here, in our deep.
        We know your oxygen tanks run low.
You must return. Follow the lights.
We are coming.
We have slept a long time.
      Since the waters were chartered.
        Since the boats stopped fearing the monstrous deep.
      Since men believed the ocean was theirs.
We have slept a long time.
Our many limbs entangled with each other.
Our grotesque bodies no more than shadows in the deep.
Our gills drifting open, closed, open.
      We sense you down here, in our deep.
        We know your oxygen tanks run low.
Follow the lights.
      As our eyes open,
         as our limbs stir, fins uncurling,
         we realise we are needed.
      So we will rise.
        Like the end of the world,
You must return. Follow the lights.
We are coming.
Rucking the ocean tides, throwing storms into the prows of ships.
We will remind these tiny land-goers
that here, there be monsters.
        Once, they understood the world was not theirs.
We sense you down here, in our deep.
        We know your oxygen tanks run low.
You must return. Follow the lights.
We are coming.
      We rise to remind you the ocean can be vengeful,
        and she can be kind.
Remember the ocean is not your property.

The octopus holds you gently
        She will guide you to the surface.
Follow the lights. We are coming.
            Know that the memory of you beats
                in the three hearts of the octopus.
                In the tide of the ocean. In the future.
See yourself—your whole self—in the octopus' eyes as you rise.

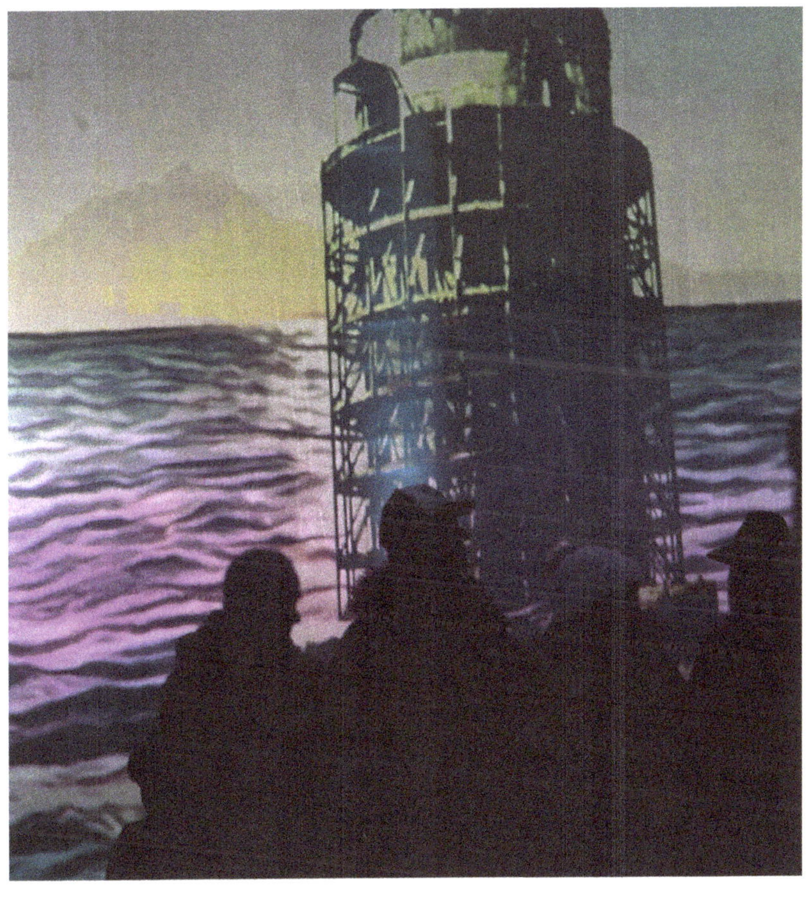

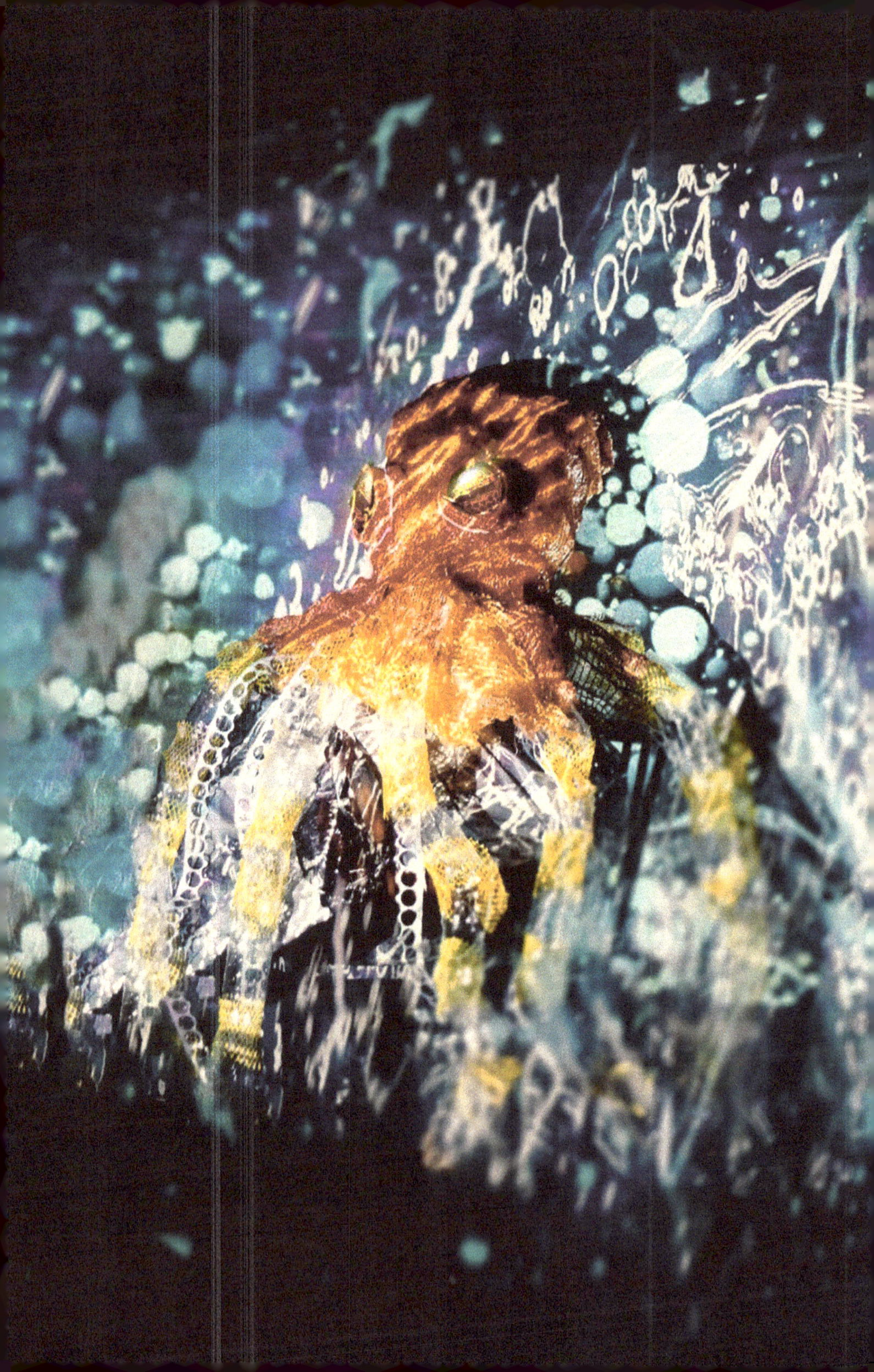

The Ocean is Waking up says the Octopus & Other Sea Creatures!

Download or stream three short audio-poems from Octopus Medicine a collection of verse-stories written by poet and performer Becci Louise. They tell a story in three parts taking us from birth to final epiphany, as we learn how a young octopus goes on an unexpected journey to discover its true potential. These stories explore themes that should resonate with us all. They investigate our relationship to the marine environment and question the way in which humankind casts nature as monstrous at a time when our impact on the planet is increasingly threatening our own existence

Octopus Medicine Audio-Poems

1. An Octopus Mother's Last Prayer for Her Hatchling (2'13") – Deep in a coral reef, guarding her eggs, an old octopus mother relays her dying advice to her babies. They will face danger everywhere.

2. An Octopus Garden (3'42") – A baby octopus explores his world, building a garden outside his lair. But what are these strange objects falling from above?
And who are the creatures that made them?

3. Beach Octopus (19'20") – Nearly an adult, the octopus discovers the shore and wants to become human. But it turns out learning to be human and learning to be a monster aren't so different.

Written and performed by: Beccy Louise
Recording, composing, and sound design: Simon Sinfield
Producer: Paul Stevens
Executive producer: Roy Hanney

Supported using public funding by the National Lottery through Arts Council England.

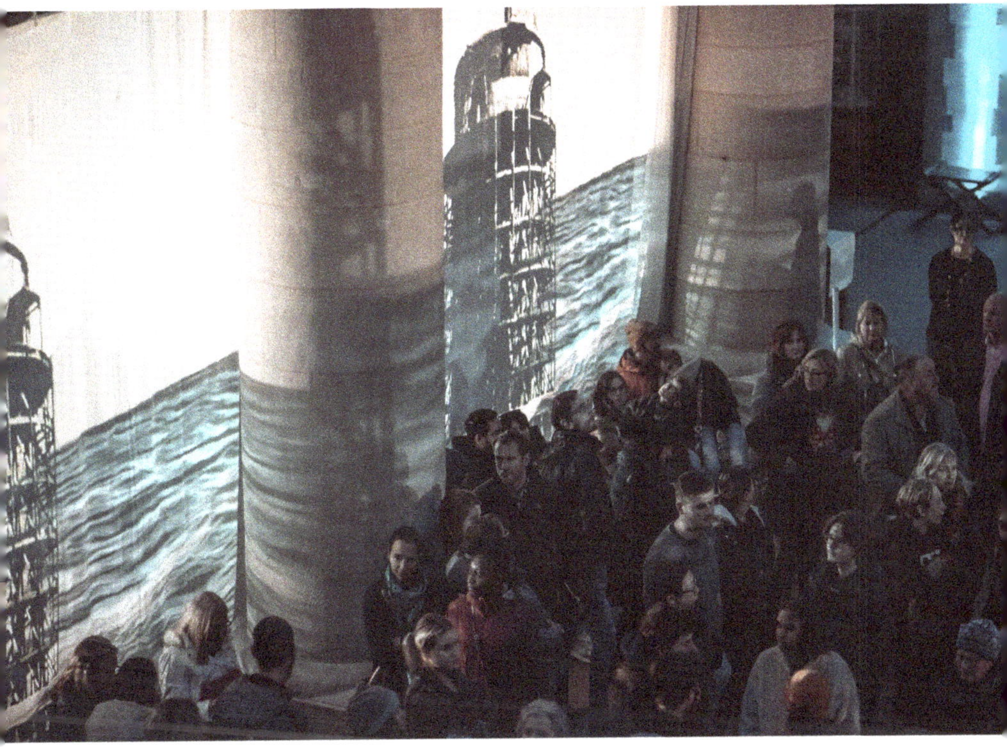

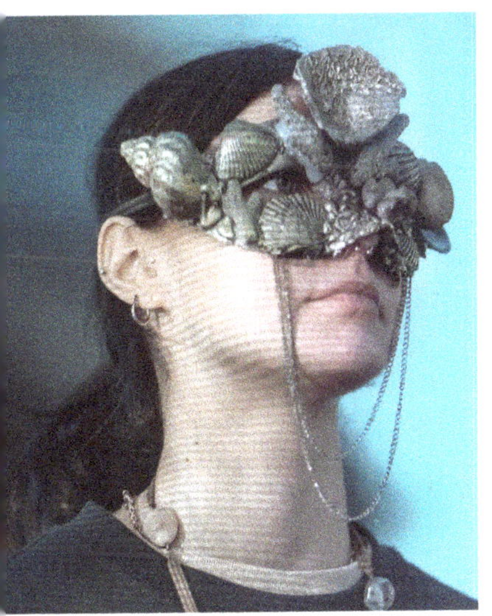

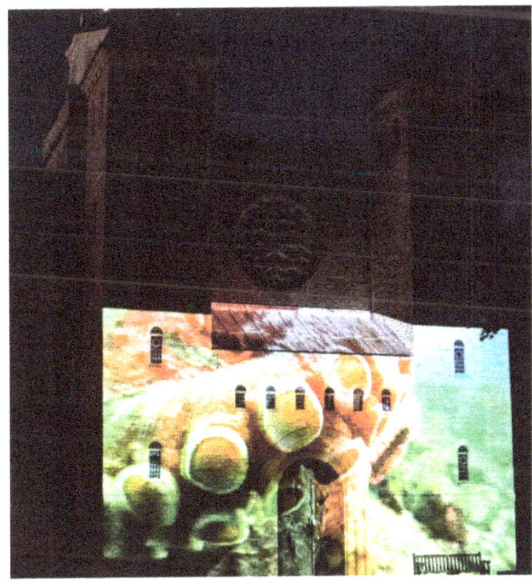

Thank you to everyone who took part, supporters and funders

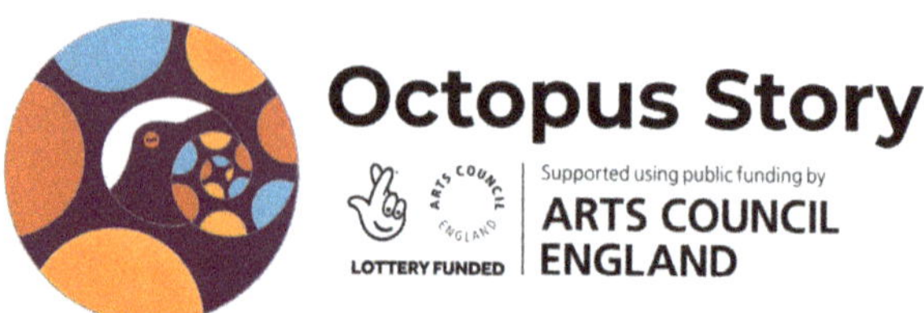

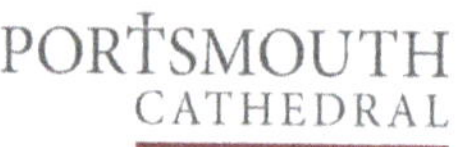
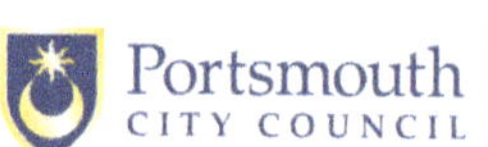
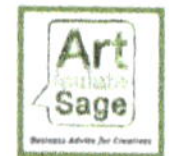

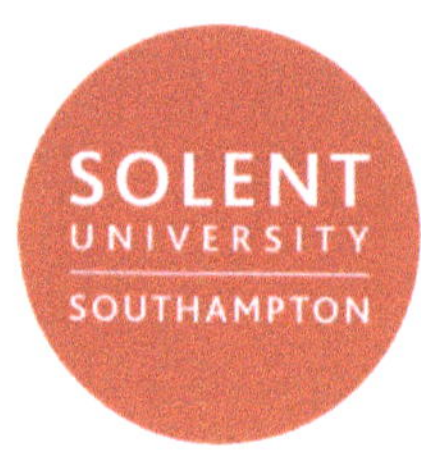